What is a Mantra?

A mantra is a short, easy-to-remember phrase that, if you repeat it to yourself, will help remind you how to positively respond to and cope with a specific situation you may find yourself in. This makes mantras excellent tools for helping you to prepare for, and deal with, anything life has to throw at you. In addition, if you use the right kind of mantras on a regular basis, they will help you build a better brain equipped with some really useful tools that will help you to have a more positive view of life, and that will help you deal with almost any situation you may encounter.

What's in this Workbook?

This workbook contains twelve different mantras. Each one has been carefully created based on the results of the latest research into human psychology to help you develop a different mental tool to cope with a type of situation that children might otherwise find difficult to deal with. This makes each one very useful on its own, but when they are all brought together, these mantras form a mental tool kit that will help you achieve more of whatever you wish to achieve, cope better with any obstacles you may encounter, and leave you feeling more relaxed and happier than you would be if you didn't have these tools available to you. Each one is accompanied by the opportunity to try it out by drawing a picture of yourself using it, or completing a short conversation you might have based on it. This will help you better understand how and when to use it.

    Once you have worked through the mantras in this book, and learned a bit about why they are useful, why they work and how you can use them to help you in your everyday life, you'll mostly likely find that you want to start coming up with your own mantras to help you deal with situations that are more specific to your life. This is a great idea, and space is provided at end where you can add your own mantras to help you personalise your mental tool kit and adapt it to your own individual needs.

Mantra One

"I can't do that ... Yet!"

When Should I Use It?

Use this mantra whenever you find yourself thinking that you can't do something, or when you've tried to do something new and you didn't manage to do it right away.

How Does It Help?

This mantra reminds you that just because you cannot do something now, it doesn't mean that you'll never be able to do it. In particular, even if you find that you can't do something the first time you try it (or the second, or the third, or even the 100th), if you keep trying, you'll get it eventually. Sometimes you may have to take a break and come back to it later before you finally succeed, but this is okay.

How Can I Practice Using It?

You can practice using this mantra by playing a game with a friend or family member. Take it in turns to ask each other whether you can do something. Make that something as weird, wild and wacky as possible, such as *'Can you juggle with jelly?'* or *'Can you put makeup on a monkey?'*. No matter what it is, the person being asked the question has to answer *'I can't do that ... Yet!'*

Mantras
To Help Kids Win At Life

> Every mistake I make is an opportunity to learn something new.

> No matter what happens, I can find a way to handle it.

> I won't decide until I've tried.

> I can't do that ... Yet!

> It's my body, what I say goes.

> Will I still think I need it tomorrow?

> Normal is just a more popular kind of being weird.

Colin M. Drysdale
Pictish Beast Publications

Text Copyright © 2019 Colin M. Drysdale
Imprint and Layout Copyright © 2019 Colin M. Drysdale/Pictish Beast Publications

All rights reserved.
No part of this book shall be reproduced, stored in a retrieval system, or transmitted by any means, electronic, mechanical, photocopying, recording, or otherwise without permission from the author.

If you wish to use any of the contents of this book for educational purposes, including photocopying individual pages to create handouts for use in classrooms, an educational licence, which allows you to legally do this, can be purchased from *www.pictishbeastpublications.com/for-educators*.

Alternatively, you can purchase a copy of our dedicated Classroom Edition (ISBN - 978-1-909832-73-2) which is in an A4 format and includes the right to photocopy its pages to create classroom handouts.

ISBN - 978-1-909832-72-5
Published by Pictish Beast Publications, Glasgow, UK.
Published in the United Kingdom
First Printing: 2019. First Edition.

The cover image is copyright © C.M. Drysdale/Pictish Beast Publications

www.PictishBeastPublications.com

Draw a picture of yourself thinking this mantra while faced with something that you don't know how to do. This could be something as ordinary as riding a bicycle or tying your shoelaces for yourself, or something as extraordinary as flying an aeroplane or climbing a massive mountain.

Mantra Two
"Smell the flower ... Blow out the candle."

When Should I Use It?

Use this mantra whenever you feel yourself getting worried, nervous, anxious or upset. This mantra isn't meant to be said out loud, rather it is one you say silently to yourself in your head. As you say the first part, breathe in slowly and deeply through your nose as if you're smelling a flower, then hold your breath for a second before breathing out again, just as slowly, through your mouth, as if you're trying to gently blow out a candle while you say the second part.

How Does It Help?

When you are worried, nervous, anxious or upset, your body reacts by entering what is known as a flight-or-fight state. This causes your heart to race and your breathing to become rapid and shallow. Our brains interpret this as meaning that something dangerous is about to happen (even if it's not), and as a result we feel anxious. This mantra works by slowing down your breathing. This, in turn, causes your body to respond by leaving the flight-or-fight state and entering a much more calm and relaxed one. This tells your brain that everything is fine and it is okay for it to relax.

How Can I Practice Using It?

The best way to practice this mantra is to set aside a few minutes at the same time each day, such as when you first wake up in the morning, when you get in from school or just before you go to bed at night. During this time, find yourself a quiet spot (like your bedroom), and turn off any distractions, such as the TV or music. Make yourself as comfortable as possible and then repeat this mantra to yourself in your head while breathing in and out as instructed. Concentrate on your breathing, and see if you can feel the effect it is having on your body. By practicing this mantra on a regular basis, you'll find it becomes much easier to use it when you really need it.

Beneath the thought bubble on the left, draw a picture yourself smelling a flower, and then beneath the right hand one, draw a picture of you blowing out a candle.

Mantra Three

"No matter what happens, I can find a way to handle it."

When Should I Use It?

Use this mantra any time you are feeling worried or nervous about what might happen next, whether that's in a few minutes time or years into the future. This mantra is best used in conjunction with mantra two (*'Smell the flower, blow out the candle'*).

How Does It Help?

From time to time, everyone worries about what might happen in the future. This is completely normal. However, when they enter your head, these types of worries can sometimes grow and multiply until they squeeze out all other thoughts. When this happens, it can cause you to panic and this can stop you from doing things you might otherwise want to do. Repeating this mantra to yourself not only helps bring these worries back under control, it can also stop them from spreading in the first place. This helps keep your mind clear and free to think about things more rationally. This gives you the mental space to come up with a well-thought out strategy for dealing with the situation you were worrying about. This mantra is especially effective when used with the deep and slow breathing pattern associated with mantra two.

How Can I Practice Using It?

You can practice using this mantra by sitting down with a friend or family member. Take turns in coming up with as wild and bizarre situations as possible, such as *'Could you handle finding a lion under your bed?'* or *'Could you handle being asked to sing for the Queen?'*. No matter what the situation you are presented with, you always reply *'No matter what happens, I can find a way to handle it.'* The person presenting the situation then asks *'How?'*, and you then have to come up with a strategy of how you would deal with it.

Think of a really weird situation that you imagine you might find difficult to handle, and then draw a picture of yourself saying this mantra when you are faced with it.

Mantra Four

"It's my body, what I say goes."

When Should I Use It?

Use this mantra when you feel that someone, whether they are another child or an adult, is invading your personal space or is trying to make you do something that makes you feel uncomfortable.

How Does It Help?

We all have an invisible bubble around us that defines our personal space. This mantra reminds you that each of us has the right to say who is allowed to enter this personal space, and who is not. It also reminds you that you have the right to say no if someone tries to enter your personal space without asking you first or getting your permission. This applies to everyone, regardless of whether they are kids or adults, friends, strangers or even relatives.

How Can I Practice Using It?

You can practice using this mantra by playing a simple game with a friend or family member. One person starts off as the body-borrower, and they ask the other person if they can borrow a part of their body (like a nose, or an ear, or a little toe). The other person tells them no. The would-be borrower then asks why, and the other person replies (in a loud voice): *'It's my body, what I say goes!'*

Think of a part of your body a body-borrower might want to borrow and write it in the first speech bubble. Once you have done this, practice using this mantra to respond to their request.

Mantra Five
"Will I still think I need it tomorrow?"

When Should I Use It?

Use this mantra when you find yourself thinking that you really, really must have something, such as a particular toy, computer game or to go to a specific event.

How Does It Help?

Our brains are wired in such a way that when we first encounter something new, we see it as incredibly desirable and we instantly want it. This feeling can, and often does, temporarily hijack our brains, driving out other, more rational thoughts. The more we give in to such instant cravings, the more intensely our brains respond in this manner, and the more difficult it becomes to control them. However, these sudden cravings are a very transient brain state, and often if we wait a little while, our brains calm down, and we can start to see that we don't really need whatever it was that initially seemed so desirable. This mantra encourages you to think about how you will view an item once your brain has returned to this calmer, more rational state. Doing this will help you to control these sudden cravings.

How Can I Practice Using It?

You can practice this mantra whenever you find yourself feeling that you really, really want something. Repeat this mantra to yourself and then make yourself wait at least a day before you do anything about your sudden want. After a day, think about the item again, and see whether you still really want it. The more often you do this, the more often you'll find that if you wait before giving in to sudden desires, they will simply evaporate.

Draw a picture of yourself looking in a shop window filled with things that you might like, but that you don't really need, and thinking of this mantra.

Mantra Six

"If I look for it, I can always find something in every day that made me happy."

When Should I Use It?

Use this mantra at the end of any day when you are feeling unhappy, when nothing seems to be going right for you, when you feel the whole world is against you, or when something bad has happened in your life.

How Does It Help?

When we are unhappy or when something bad happens in our lives, it is only natural to dwell on it. However, when we focus too much on our unhappiness or the bad things that have happened to us, and nothing else, it creates a feedback loop in our brains which makes us feel even worse. This is known as rumination, and it makes it very difficult for us to see any good in our lives. This mantra helps to remind you that no matter how bad things are, there are still good things out there too, and even on the worst of days, there will always have been something that has made you feel happy, even if it was only for a few seconds. By focusing on these good things, rather than the bad ones, it can stop your brain from becoming trapped in a state of rumination. This, in turn, allows you to focus on changing your life for the better, rather than getting stuck on focusing on the things that make you unhappy.

How Can I Practice Using It?

You can practice this mantra by doing an exercise called *Three Happy Things*. To do this exercise, sit down with a friend or family member and tell them three things about your day that made you happy. If you don't have anyone to sit down with (or if you don't want to do this), this is okay and you can write them down instead. You can also just do it in your head as you lie in bed at the end of the day before going to sleep. The more frequently you do this exercise the better, and it will have the biggest positive impact on your life if you get into the habit of doing it at least once a day.

At the end of a day, find yourself somewhere quiet and think back over everything you did, saw or that happened in it, and see if you can come up with three things that made you really happy, even if it was just for a moment. It could be something really simple like the sound of your little brother laughing or a dog licking your face, or something really big like being able to swim across the swimming pool without armbands for the very first time. Once you have thought of your three happy things, write them in the speech bubbles below.

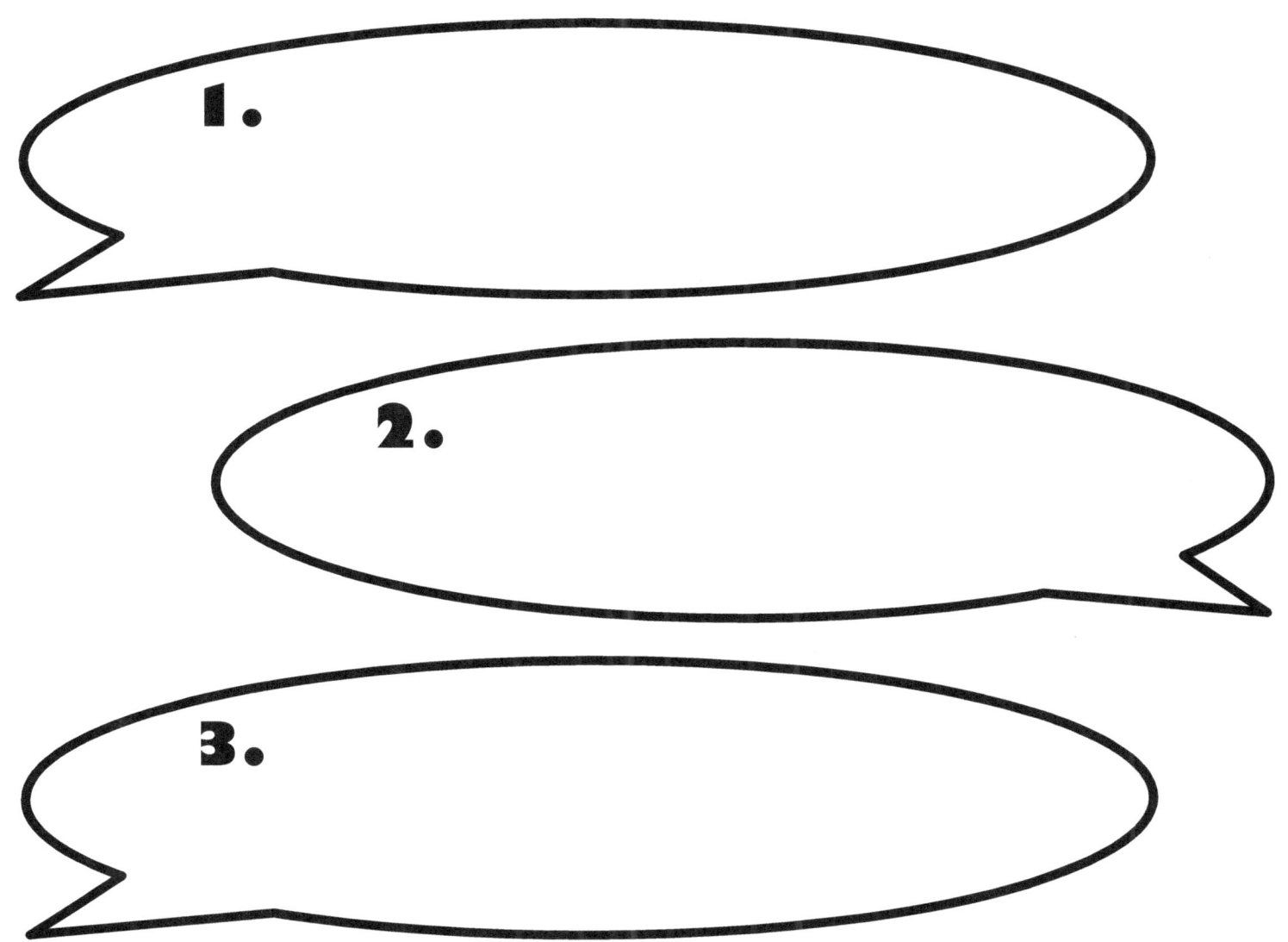

Mantra Seven

"I will try hard, be kind, and think before I do."

When Should I Use It?

Use this mantra at the start of each day, when you're going through the school gate, or just before you try anything new.

How Does It Help?

This mantra reminds you of three important things that are good habits to get into. These are trying as hard as you possibly can, being kind to yourself and to those around you, and thinking through the potential consequences of your actions before you do anything to ensure that they are appropriate for the situation that you are in. By reminding yourself of these habits on a regular basis, you are more likely to practice them, and the more you practice them, the more they will become an automatic part of your everyday life. This will help you develop what is called a growth mindset, which is a way of viewing the world that is likely to lead to you being much happier and successful in whatever you choose to do with your life.

How Can I Practice Using It?

The best way to practice this mantra is to sit down with a friend or family member and take it in turns to come up with examples of people displaying one or more of these habits. These examples can come from your own life, from the lives of your friends and family, from books you have read, TV shows you've watched or films you have seen. For each example you come up with, see if you can explain how using the habit benefitted the person either in the short or the longer term.

Draw picture of yourself leaving your house first thing in the morning, making sure that the thought bubbles for this mantra are coming out of you head.

Mantra Eight

"I won't decide until I've tried."

When Should I Use It?

Use this mantra whenever you find yourself confronted with a new or unfamiliar place, activity or situation. This might be starting at a new school, trying a new sport, going to a club for the first time, or eating something new.

How Does It Help?

It is completely normal to worry about new or unfamiliar situations. However, these worries can easily get out of hand and stop us doing things that we otherwise might wish to do. This can lead to our lives becoming very closed off from the new experiences and opportunities that allow us to grow as people. It's amazing how often something we were certain we would never, ever like, turns out to be really enjoyable once we give it a go. This mantra reminds you that you cannot let a fear of the unfamiliar stop you trying new things. After all, the worst thing that can happen when you try something new is that you find that you don't like it. In that case, you don't have to do it again. However, if you don't try it, you will never know if you'd have liked it or not, and this can lead you to missing out on some amazing opportunities. When you look back on your life, it will be the opportunities you didn't take that you'll regret more than the ones you took, even if it turned out that you didn't like doing a particular thing.

How Can I Practice Using It?

You can practice using this mantra by sitting down with a friend or family member and taking turns to ask each other if you'd like to do all sorts of weird things, like eating a worm sandwich, or drinking a slug milkshake. No matter what is asked, the other person replies, *'I won't decide until I've tried'*. The stranger the things are that you ask if a person would like to do, the funnier the game will become.

Think about something really, really wild and wacky that you've never done before, and that you imagine might not be particularly pleasant to do. Write it into the top speech bubble. Once you have done this, practice giving this mantra in response to being asked if you'd like to do it.

Mantra Nine

"Every mistake I make is an opportunity to learn something new."

When Should I Use It?

Use this mantra whenever you find yourself feeling bad because you made a mistake, or whenever you find yourself worrying that you might make one, especially if it's stopping you trying your best to do something.

How Does It Help?

Everyone makes mistakes, and making mistakes is one of the best ways of learning how to do something new. However, if we worry too much about making mistakes, or if we find ourselves feeling bad because we made one, we can end up not trying new things, and not pushing ourselves to reach our full potential. This is not to say that some mistakes are not bad, or that they might not have big consequences, but if we do our very best to learn something from every mistake we make, then we are much less likely to make the same mistake again. This mantra helps you change the way you think about the mistakes you make and see them not as bad things that must be avoided at all costs, but as part of the normal learning process. It also reminds you to make sure that you do learn from them.

How Can I Practice Using it?

You can practice using this mantra by sitting down with a friend or family member. Take it in turn to come up with a silly situation, and an amusing mistake you could make in it. The other person then has to respond by saying '*Every mistake I make is an opportunity to learn something new*', and then they must come up with a suggestion for something new they could learn from making that specific mistake.

Draw a picture of yourself making a really silly mistake, like accidently wearing your slippers to school, and then using this mantra to remind yourself that it is an opportunity to learn something new. What could you learn from accidently wearing your slippers to school?

Every mistake I make is an opportunity to learn something new!

Mantra Ten

"I measure my success against my past self, and not just against the achievements of others."

When Should I Use It?

Use this mantra whenever you find yourself comparing yourself to others when you are trying to learn something new, or improve your ability to do anything, whether at school, on the sports field or at home. This mantra is particularly useful when you are learning in a group environment.

How Does It Help?

It is always very tempting to compare yourself to those around you in order to see how well you are doing. However, this can make you feel bad if you feel you are not doing as well as everyone else. This mantra reminds you that the best person to compare yourself to, in order to see how well you are doing, is your past self as this allows you to see how far you've come. For example, if you are in a class learning to juggle, and if after a month everyone else can juggle four balls while you can only juggle three, you may feel disheartened if you only compare yourself to those around you. However, if you also compare yourself to how you were a month ago (when you couldn't juggle at all), you'll be able to see that you can now juggle much better than before. This is much more rewarding and will help encourage you to keep going until you, too, can juggle four balls at once.

How Can I Practice Using It?

The best way to practice this mantra is to think of a situation where you regularly find yourself comparing your success to those around you rather than to your past self. This might be when you get the results of your homework back, when you have a test at school, when practising sports, or when playing with your friends. Once you have identified such a situation, set yourself the target of repeating this mantra to yourself every time you find yourself in it from now on. This will help the ideas behind it become an automatic part of your way of thinking about measuring your achievements.

On the left hand side of this page, draw a picture of yourself as a little baby, and then draw a picture of yourself today on the right hand side. Think about three things you can do now that you couldn't do when you were younger and write them in the thought bubbles.

Mantra Eleven

"I can't control the actions of others, but I can control how I respond to them."

When Should I Use It?

Use this mantra whenever you find yourself feeling frustrated, angry or hurt by the behaviour of others, regardless of whether they are friends, classmates, family members, or even strangers that you don't know.

How Does It Help?

This mantra reminds you of two important things. Firstly, no matter how much you may wish you could, you cannot control how other people behave, and trying to do so will just leave you feeling angry and frustrated. Secondly, what you can control is how you respond to their actions. If you can remain calm and in control when someone else is trying to annoy you or wind you up, you'll not only feel better about it (because you have remained in control), you will also often find that they stop doing it because they are not getting the response they were looking for. This works particularly well in situations where someone is trying to bully you. However, it also works in situations where someone's unthinking actions impact you accidentally rather than on purpose. The aim here is not to change how the other persons actions make you feel (such as feeling frustrated, angry or hurt) as these are often valid feelings, but only how you respond so that you remain in control of your actions rather than lashing out at those around you.

How Can I Practice Using It?

You can practice this mantra by sitting down with a friend or family member. Take turns in suggesting the actions of others that might frustrate, anger or hurt you. Respond by saying *'I can't control the actions of others, but I can control how I respond.'* The other person then asks *'How would you respond?'*, and you then need to come up with a way to respond to that situation which would reflect how the situation would make you feel, but that wouldn't result in you losing control as a result of these feelings.

Think of an action that someone else might do that you'd find really frustrating and write this in the top speech bubble. Now think of a way you could respond which would reflect how the situation would make you feel, but that wouldn't result in you losing control as a result of these feelings. Write this response in the speech bubble at the bottom of the page.

Mantra Twelve

"Normal is just a more popular kind of being weird."

When Should I Use It?

Use this mantra whenever you find yourself thinking that you are weird or that you don't fit in with those around you.

How Does It Help?

This mantra reminds you that there is no such thing as being normal, that everyone is an individual, and that, when you think about it, everyone is weird in some way or other. The important thing is that you need to be your own kind of weird, and not the kind of weird you think someone else thinks you should be just because they call it normal. After all, it's better to be your own kind of weird and happy, than to pretend to be something you're not, as this can leave you feeling very unhappy.

How Can I Practice Using It?

The best way to practice this mantra is to play a game with a friend or family member. One of you starts by saying *'Normal people ...'* before completing the sentence with something they consider normal (for example *'Normal people like watching football'*). The other then replies, *'But that's weird because ...'* and completes the sentence with a reason why this thing that other people might consider normal is, when you stop and think about it, actually a bit weird. In the example above, about watching football, you might respond by saying *'But that's weird because all they're doing is watching a bunch of people who get paid a lot of money chase a small ball around a large field.'*

Draw a picture of yourself saying this mantra as you do something that you think is normal, but draw yourself wearing clothes that people wouldn't usually wear for doing it. This could be wearing a fairy princess costume to play football, wearing your best clothes to go swimming, or wearing your pyjamas to school!

Normal is just a more popular kind of being weird

Make Up Your Own Mantras

Mantras are a great way of summarising any lessons you learn from life. This means it's useful (and fun) to come up with your very own mantras that are specific to your own personal life. You can use this space, and the space on the next page, to add any mantras you come up with that you find useful. Once you have done this, see if you can come up with any games you could play to help you practice them.

Additional Information For Grown-ups

The mantras in this workbook are most useful when they become a part of your child's everyday life. This means it is important that they both practice them regularly, and that they apply them whenever an appropriate situation arises. You can help with both of these, but at all times make sure that you do it in a non-judgemental and constructive manner. In particular, don't try to force your child to adopt them, and resist the urge to instantly leap in and correct your child if you feel that they are using them inappropriately. Instead, give them the opportunity, and the time, to work this out for themselves, and if they don't, try to lead them gently towards this realisation. This is because the more they feel that working with mantras comes from themselves, rather than being forced on them by the adults in their lives, the more they will benefit from them, both now, and for the rest of their lives.

The same applies when encouraging children to come up with their own personal mantras to summarise lessons they've learned from their own experiences. Let them take the lead, and pick their own mantras. In addition, try to let them learn their own lessons from their own experiences, rather than trying to force lessons on them that you think they should learn from any given situation. However, you may have to help them with the exact phrasing to ensure their mantras provide them with the most appropriate and positive message. More information on the types of phrasing to use, or to avoid, when creating your own mantras is provided on the next page.

Finally, when you observe your child spontaneously using a mantra in an appropriate situation, make sure that you let them know that you noticed it, and provide them with positive, enthusiastic praise that specifically highlights to them what they did, and why it was good. This will help them understand how to apply the mantras in this book to help them in their everyday lives.

If you wish to find out more about the science and psychology behind these mantras, a brief outline of the five key psychological principles on which they are based can be found at the end of this book, along with a suggestion for further reading, if you wish to delve into any of them in greater detail. However, do not feel that you have to do this – it is purely optional!

Phrasing To Use And To Avoid When Creating Your Own Mantras

The exact phrasing used for a mantra can have a big impact on its effectiveness in helping your child expand and develop their mental tool kit. This may, at first, make working with your child to come up with their own mantras seem a little daunting, there are a few simple rules which, if you follow them, will allow you to create the best possible mantras to help your child cope with any given situation. These rules are:

1. It is better if mantras are worded in the first person (me or I) rather than the second person (you) or the third person (he/she/people). This will encourage your child to embrace the mantra and the message it contains.

2. Avoid the use of words like Should/Shouldn't and Must/Mustn't. This is because these words can make children feel like they are doing something because they are being told to, rather than that they are doing it for themselves and for their own benefit. Instead, use words like Will or Won't, as these encourage children to take ownership of the mantra.

3. Try to make sure that all mantras are worded in such a way that they focus on encouraging positive actions rather than preventing negatives ones. This is because children tend to focus on the types of actions they hear the most about, and this means that positive mantras encourage positive behaviours, while negative ones risk focusing too much attention on negative behaviours.

4. Make sure that mantras are worded in such a way that they focus on behaviours and responses, rather than on the fundamental characteristics of your child and who they are as a person. This is because mantras that focus on what the child perceives to be unalterable characteristics can have a negative effect on them if they fail to live up to them. For example, when trying to encourage a child to think about the impact of their actions on others, simply getting them to say '*I am a kind person*' will set them up for failure as there are always times when, for whatever reason, they will find themselves acting in an unkind way. In contrast, if they use the mantra '*be kind*', this reinforces that they should try to act in a kind and considerate manner, but it doesn't set them up for failure if there are occasions when they find themselves not being as kind as they could be to themselves or to those around them.

5. Try to ensure that mantras are worded in a way that is consistent with your child's personality and who they feel they are. This will increase the likelihood that your child will include them in their own personal mental tool kit.
6. Try to make sure that any mantras your child comes up with do not result in them prioritising the well-being of others over their own well-being. For example, the mantra *'I shouldn't hurt the feelings of others'* will likely encourage a child to avoid hurting others at all costs, even if it is detrimental to their own well-being, and this is not a positive outcome. In contrast, *'I will try to be considerate of the feelings of others'* has the same general meaning, but it allows for situations where a child needs to put their own feelings above those of others, if that is what is best in a specific instance.

The Science Behind Using These Mantras In Everyday Life

The mantras in this workbook have been created using a range of psychological principles, with the aim of helping children apply them to their lives in a simple and straight forward manner. Foremost amongst these are five inter-related elements. These are growth mindset theory, cognitive behaviour therapy, the chimp mind management model, nudge theory, and wise psychological interventions.

1. **Growth Mindset Theory:** Growth mindset theory is the idea that the way we perceive problems we encounter is a more important factor in determining whether we will solve them than any innate abilities. In short, if we believe that we are capable of solving a problem by working hard at it, we are much more likely to be able to do so than if we believe that the ability to solve any particular problem is down to some sort of innate talent that we were born with. Building on this basic tenet, the mantras in this workbook aim to encourage children to see their abilities not as something that were fixed at birth, but as something that they can develop over time, and that it is within their power to choose how these abilities develop. If you wish to learn more about growth mindset theory, you can read *Mindset: How You Can Fulfil Your Potential* by Carol Dweck.

2. **Cognitive Behavioural Therapy (CBT):** Cognitive behavioural therapy, or CBT for short, is an approach which encourages people to deal with problems they face by changing the way that they think about them, and so how they respond to them. While CBT requires a level of self-awareness and self-examination that most children simply do not have, the mantras in this workbook encourage children to respond to specific situations in a psychologically positive manner that will provide a firm foundation for their future psychological development. This, in turn, encourages them to look at any issues they may encounter in their lives in such a way that they feel they have the mental tools to work out how best to respond to them. If you wish to learn more about cognitive behavioural therapy, you can read *Change Your Thinking: Positive and Practical Ways To Overcome Stress, Negative Emotions and Self-defeating Behaviour Using CBT* by Sarah Edelman.

3. **Chimp Mind Management Model:** The chimp mind management model was developed by Professor Steve Peters as a way to help people understand how their brains work, and how they can program them to react in a conscious, positive and logical manner rather than in the instinctive, emotional way that is the default within the human brain. One of the best ways to do this is to provide pre-considered routines of how to react to different situations. This, then, provides a set of mental tools that we can use to help us deal with the challenges we face in our everyday lives. While relatively simple, the mantras in this workbook have been specifically created to provide children with tools that they can apply to situations they are likely to encounter in their daily lives both as children and as adults. These include things like making mistakes, running into difficulties in completing a specific task, and self-confidence. Thus, taken as a whole, the mantras in this workbook provide a tool set that helps children deal with all that life may throw at them in a positive, conscious and logical manner. If you wish to learn more about the chimp mind management model, you can read *The Chimp Paradox: The Mind Management Programme To Help You Achieve Success, Confidence and Happiness* by Professor Steve Peters.

4. **Nudge Theory:** Nudge theory is the idea that, if chosen carefully, relatively small changes in the way that information is presented to a person can have large positive impacts on their actions. For this workbook, this means that the wording of the mantras included in it have been specifically chosen to give the highest likelihood that the positive message behind them will be understood by children and will be incorporated into their own personal set of mind management tools. This gives the greatest chance that these tool will be available when they are needed. If you wish to learn more about nudge theory, you can read *Nudge: Improving Decisions about Health, Wealth, and Happiness* by Cass Sunstein and Richard Thaler.

5. **Wise Psychological Interventions (WPIs):** WPIs are a relatively new area of psychology, but the principle behind them is very straight forward and can be thought of as building on nudge theory. WPI theory states that is it not enough to simply provide a person with a useful piece of information that will benefit them, it also has to be presented to them at just the right time in order to have the biggest possible positive impact. In fact, WPI research suggests that the right thing presented to a person in the right way at just the right time can have large, and long-lasting, positive impacts upon them and their psychology. Each mantra in this workbook has

been designed to be just the right thing presented in just the right way to help children develop a positive mental tool for use in a specific circumstance that they are likely to encounter in their everyday life. However, the trouble with applying WPI theory to child development is that it can be very difficult to identify when an individual child will most benefit from receiving a specific piece of advice or information, especially when if comes in the form of a psychological tool. This issue has been dealt with for the mantras in this workbook by providing advice on how best to practice them. If the mantras are practised regularly, this will mean that they will already be available to the child at the moment when they have the potential to have the biggest impact upon them and their psychological development. If you wish to learn more about wise psychological interventions, you can read this article from *New Scientist* magazine: *https://www.newscientist.com/ article/2080024-wise-interventions-when-your-brain-needs-a-stronger-nudge/.*

www.ingramcontent.com/pod-product-compliance
Lightning Source LLC
Chambersburg PA
CBHW081130080526
44587CB00021B/3814